He Waits for Me

LOVE LETTERS FROM THE LORD

ISBN: 978-1-7342592-0-9

Cover art and book design by Meagan Vanderhill
Cover photo by Artem Kovalev

my deepest thanks

To my Savior, Lord, and Friend—King Jesus. You saved me. You brought me back to life, and for that, I will forever rest at Your feet in deepest praise and gratitude. You alone are worthy. I adore You, and I'm eternally Yours.

To my Mom and Dad who consistently spoke life into a little girl's heart that she had a gift to write, thank you. You've always believed in me and encouraged me to pursue this dream. I am eternally grateful. I love you both so much.

To my prayer warriors—Toni G., Sara G., Jill G., Hana C., Jessie C., Juliana S., Ashley W., Marcie M.; your prayer covering has meant the world to me. Thank you for always checking in and faithfully going to the Father with me. I couldn't imagine having anyone else by my side. I love you all.

To my friend and spiritual mom, Pastor Lyn O., your unapologetic teaching of the gospel has helped set me free in more ways than I can express. Thank you for opening your heart and your house to me. I love you.

To my friend and partner in this project, Meagan V., you've managed to capture everything I was looking for in the cover, layout and little details —all with little to no help from me. You have a gift, my friend, and I know your work will bless so many. Forever grateful for you.

And to so many others who have spoken words of encouragement into my life over the years, you will forever hold a piece of my heart and highest appreciation.

introduction

Dear Reader,

I want you to know that I've been praying for you. I know we may not know each other, but you've been on my heart as I prayed for each and every person who would hold this book in their hands. I don't know what your journey with Jesus looks like, but if it is anything like mine then I know you need the truths within these pages just as much as I do.

This collection of letters is meant to be poured over and chewed on (metaphorically speaking), until it becomes a reality in the way you see yourself and the love God has for you. There are 30 letters, one for each day of the month, which are written to you. Each one a declaration of truth and love, and invitations to go deeper into relationship with Jesus.

You can use this book any way you choose, but here are just a few suggestions to help you get started:

1. As a daily devotional: Read one letter each day and journal your thoughts and prayers over what you've read. Write out the scripture verses that accompany each letter.

2. As a biblical meditation guide: Read the letters and scriptures that apply to areas you need breakthrough; then recite the biblical truths over and over (meditating) until they replace the lies that war against what God says about you and His love for you.

3. A recurring devotional: Revisit the letters down the road after you've completed each one and see how you've grown in your understanding of who He's created you to be. Journal your new insights and understandings of the scriptures.

There is one additional letter at the end of this book that is my own love letter to the Lord. It shares a bit of my testimony and journey with our good-good God. After reading my letter, you will be invited to write your own love letter to Him as a practice of praise, worship, and thanksgiving.

However you decide to utilize this devotional, full of declarations of love and identity, is up to you. I pray that it blesses you abundantly more than you could ever ask or imagine. I pray that you know you are precious in His sight, and you are dear to me.

You are so deeply loved.

With all my heart,

Tillany

number one

ROMANS 1:20

My Child, I come dancing on the bright rays of the sun shining through your windows. My fingerprints, My divine nature, are hidden in the little details of the beauty all around you. Oh, how I love to create!

I thought of you, you know; when I designed each tender petal on every flower. Each one clothed in color cascading across the gardens. I thought of your eyes as they would widen and take in the brilliance of the sight before you, and how your spirit would know that all of this was designed to point your eyes to Me.

My Love, listen to the melody of sounds that come together in a crescendo through the air as the birds call out in their unique voices, and the leaves rustle and sway as the breaths of wind pass through. I was intentional with every single detail, My Love, because I wanted you to know My Presence. I want My image bearers to see My Presence all around them.

I spoke a word and My love poured out into a glorious display all around. Consider My creation My very first love letter to you, My Beloved.

Take some time to reflect on these truths with Holy Spirit. How have you seen this in your own life and walk with God? What areas do you want to experience more of it? Ask Him to reveal more of Himself to you today.

number two

ROMANS 3:21–23, JOHN 15:2

My Child, yes, you are Mine. I see you striving and trying with all your might to be 'good', but that isn't how I designed a relationship with Me. Complete righteousness was accomplished by My Son.

Willpower and good works will never earn you righteousness. You became righteous the moment you put your faith in My Son. Self-control is a fruit of My Spirit at work within you, and it can only come through a surrendered heart.

Because you are Mine, I Am the one who will create the deep changes within you. I will never stop molding and shaping your character to mirror the image of My Son. Your part in this process is simply to surrender control.

So come to Me, Beloved, as a dearly loved child runs to a deeply devoted Father—swiftly and without question of their acceptance.

Let go and let Me work. Lean in and seek My face while you rest in My arms. Receive My love. Allow Me to strengthen your spirit and prune away the unnecessary so that the essential can grow and produce fruit.

You are My child and I love you. Rest in Me and trust what I am doing in and through you.

Take some time to reflect on these truths with Holy Spirit. How have you seen this in your own life and walk with God? What areas do you want to experience more of it? Ask Him to reveal more of Himself to you today.

number three

1 CORINTHIANS 6:19, 1 KINGS 19:11–13

My Child, why do you look around as if I am not here? I've never left you. My greatest desire has always been to be with you. Do you not know that your very being is the Temple in which My Holy Spirit resides?

I came to live within you the very moment you confessed with your mouth and believed in your heart that I Am LORD of all. You carry Me with you always, nothing and no one can separate us. I wait in great anticipation every day for our conversations with one another. I have so much I want to share with you, and if you lean in and listen you'll hear Me whisper to your Spirit the way in which you should go.

I'll never force you to do anything, I honor your gift of free-will, given to you by Me. I only seek your genuine desire to give Me your whole heart. And if you'll let Me, I'll take you on adventures you've never dreamt or imagined possible. Take My hand and walk by faith with Me, I'll light the way.

Take some time to reflect on these truths with Holy Spirit. How have you seen this in your own life and walk with God? What areas do you want to experience more of it? Ask Him to reveal more of Himself to you today.

number four

MATTHEW 18:3

My Child, close your eyes with Me for a moment and remember a time when you were at play. Can you see it? This is the version of you I see when I look at you. You are full of faith and trust, completely in the moment and overflowing with joy. This is My desire for you, My Love, this is how I created you to be. You were never meant to 'grow up' and lose your sense of wonder and awe. Your sense of timelessness and complete trust, that no matter what, if you jump, I will catch you.

All of this is how I designed you to live.

Only this child-like faith can open your eyes to the Kingdom. It's in you, right now, at this very moment. You haven't lost it, all you need is to ask Me to breathe life back into it.

Come, My Child, it's time to live in a sense of wonder once again.

Take some time to reflect on these truths with Holy Spirit. How have you seen this in your own life and walk with God? What areas do you want to experience more of it? Ask Him to reveal more of Himself to you today.

number five

GENESIS 1:26–28, PSALM 139:14

My Child, do you know how unique you are? There has never been a single person to walk this earth that is, or was, exactly like you. Even identical twins aren't exactly the same.

Do you know why I created each of my children so uniquely? Because each and every one of you holds a piece of My image. When you look at your reflection in the mirror, when you look into another persons' eyes; you see a part of Me.

So when you look at another with eyes of comparison, you are missing out on the rarity that is you, only you. No one else will ever contain what you have. Only you can release what I've placed in you into the world around you. You were created with great attention to detail and immense purpose. Don't miss out on how special you are My Child by wishing you were something or someone else. You were made for such a time as this and I Am with you in every step.

See yourself through My eyes, you are a wonder to behold.

You are fearfully and wonderfully made by Me, and I love what I see.

Take some time to reflect on these truths with Holy Spirit. How have you seen this in your own life and walk with God? What areas do you want to experience more of it? Ask Him to reveal more of Himself to you today.

number six

**JOHN 3:16–17, 1 JOHN 2:9–10, 1 JOHN 4:18–19,
1 CORINTHIANS 13:4–8, ROMANS 12:9–10**

My Child, I want you to practice seeing the people around you today with My eyes. I want to give you My eyes to see the beauty and complexity of each individual. Not one of them is the same as the other. Most importantly, each individual heart is extremely precious to Me.

I see what's inside each one, and still, I love them. Even when they don't love Me back, I love them unconditionally. Love is a choice, and you must choose love every day—every time you interact with one another.

I will help you, you won't be able to do this without Me. I Am Love, to know Me is to know True Love. And only through your intimacy with Me will you be able to love one another.

Abide in Me, I'll give you eyes to see and a heart that loves without fear.

Take some time to reflect on these truths with Holy Spirit. How have you seen this in your own life and walk with God? What areas do you want to experience more of it? Ask Him to reveal more of Himself to you today.

number seven

1 JOHN 4:17–19, PSALM 91

My Child, when you are afraid, remember I AM with you always! I Am Almighty God. I Am Perfect Love, fear cannot stand in My Presence. Do not allow fear to intimidate you, you are My Child and you carry My Presence and authority. I fight for you always! The moment you call My Name, you call down heaven.

I command My angels to stand guard over you. You do not need to fear the enemy, he cannot touch you. Keep your eyes on Me, My Child, I Am the Light and the darkness cannot overcome Me. Choose to use the arrival of fear as a reminder that this is an opportunity to watch Me move mightily on your behalf!

Call out My Name. You are wrapped up tight, closely guarded and covered by My Presence. Be still and know that I Am your God.

Take some time to reflect on these truths with Holy Spirit. How have you seen this in your own life and walk with God? What areas do you want to experience more of it? Ask Him to reveal more of Himself to you today.

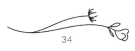

HEBREWS 4:15, ROMANS 5:20, ISAIAH 58:11

My Child, there is nothing on this earth you'll walk through, that I haven't experienced Myself. Lean on Me, Beloved, and let Me guide you through.

Every day, every new situation, is an opportunity for you to experience My love for you in new and higher ways. My grace abounds towards you, it's always pouring out.

Do you see it?

Do you sense it?

The power of My Presence to impact your life, to strengthen you and bring you peace. I Am always available to you. Turn your eyes towards Me, My Love, and you will find Me.

Take some time to reflect on these truths with Holy Spirit. How have you seen this in your own life and walk with God? What areas do you want to experience more of it? Ask Him to reveal more of Himself to you today.

number nine

JOHN 5:19, ECCLESIASTES 3:1–8, ROMANS 8:28

My Child, follow My example displayed during My time on earth, I was never in a hurry. I only did what the Father did, and I only spoke what the Father spoke. Everything else was unnecessary.

I stole away often to commune with our Father, to worship Him and to receive His guidance. This is what you were created for.

Kingdom purpose, My timing, is never rushed—it's perfect. Everything happens in its time. Never before, never late—always exactly as it should be.

There is never a moment in time that I am not at work on your behalf. Even if you can't see it, things are in motion. I am for you, My plans for you are good! So rest in the truth of Who I am and that nothing is impossible for Me, Beloved. I am outside of space and time, I see all things—so trust My timing and come to Me. I have so much I want to share with you as you sit in My Presence.

Take some time to reflect on these truths with Holy Spirit. How have you seen this in your own life and walk with God? What areas do you want to experience more of it? Ask Him to reveal more of Himself to you today.

number ten

PSALM 46:10, EXODUS 14:14, EPHESIANS 2:6

My Child, let Me fight for you. Do you not know that you are seated with Me in the heavenlies? Yes, seated in a posture of victory next to Me, the Undefeated One. You live from victory, but you are acting like you are trying to attain it. Don't forget who and Whose you are.

Rest child, stop fighting. Rest, and lay your burdens down upon Me. I Am strong enough to carry them, you were never designed to bear that kind of weight. You were designed to be free and worship Me.

I Am your Shelter from the storm. Come now My Child and rest in Me.

Take some time to reflect on these truths with Holy Spirit. How have you seen this in your own life and walk with God? What areas do you want to experience more of it? Ask Him to reveal more of Himself to you today.

LOVE LETTER

number eleven

PROVERBS 16:9, 1 CORINTHIANS 1:9,
1 JOHN 1:3, 1 CORINTHIANS 12:13

My Child, why are you striving? I see you exerting so much effort. I hear you saying, "If it is to be then it is up to me!" This is an orphan's mentality. You are not alone, you never have been.

Don't you know who you are? You are My Child. Mine. I have amazing plans for your life and all they require is an obedient heart and a ready 'Yes' to partner with Me.

I determine your steps. I open the doors and pour My favor and blessing out over your path. My yoke is light and the burden of your calling is easy as you partner with Me, the Great I Am. I do the heavy lifting My Child, not you.

Rest in your identity as My Beloved Child and watch as My favor flows easily into your life simply because I love you. Yes, you are deeply and extravagantly loved. You are Mine, and I Am yours.

Take some time to reflect on these truths with Holy Spirit. How have you seen this in your own life and walk with God? What areas do you want to experience more of it? Ask Him to reveal more of Himself to you today.

number twelve

PSALM 116:2, HEBREWS 4:16, EPHESIANS 3:12, HEBREWS 12:2

My Child, I love the sound of your voice! It was one of the things I thought of as I endured the cross. I knew that once you were redeemed, you would have the freedom to come into My Presence and speak to Me as a beloved child … as a friend. As you pray I lean down to listen, I never miss a thing.

As you pray, our relationship grows as I show you more of My heart towards you.

As you pray in the Spirit you are strengthened through the exchange from your spirit to Mine. So much happens here in the secret place with Me, even if you can't see it.

Your prayers are treasured so profoundly that I keep each one in golden bowls next to Me. Each one precious, each one like sweet incense to Me. Never doubt My desire to hear that voice of yours, and share My heart with you in return. There is nothing you could do that could quench the longing in My heart for you.

Take some time to reflect on these truths with Holy Spirit. How have you seen this in your own life and walk with God? What areas do you want to experience more of it? Ask Him to reveal more of Himself to you today.

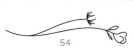

number thirteen

JOHN 3:16, 2 CHRONICLES 6:14, ROMANS 8:31–32, REVELATION 3:20, 1 CORINTHIANS 2:10

I love you. Yes, My Child, you—I love you with an everlasting love. A perfect, unfailing love. I love everything about you. Every single detail of what makes you—you, brings Me great delight. I see you as you truly are, and I love you.

There is nothing I would withhold from you, I gave you My greatest gift—My Son. So, in turn, I gave you all of Me.

Every moment of every day I am speaking to you, speaking words of love and edification. Do you hear Me?

Lean in and listen for that whisper, My still small voice. Don't doubt that you can hear it. You heard My voice the day I stood at the door of your heart and knocked, calling out to you to invite Me in.

You're My Child and I eagerly want to talk with you. Be still and listen.

Sit with Me, My Beloved, and share your heart with Me, and I'll share Mine with you.

Stay a while, I've missed you.

Take some time to reflect on these truths with Holy Spirit. How have you seen this in your own life and walk with God? What areas do you want to experience more of it? Ask Him to reveal more of Himself to you today.

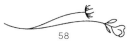

number fourteen

PSALM 23, 1 CORINTHIANS 1:9, REVELATION 3:20, ROMANS 8:1, JEREMIAH 31:25

My Child, come and dine with Me. I've seen you wandering with your eyes focused on the chaos out there. Your feet follow where your eyes are pointed. Don't look out there, look at Me.

Dine with Me. I've prepared a table full of nourishment, and fellowship, an intimate setting for just you and I. Come, join Me, Beloved!

Here, at My table, you'll discover the peace amongst the chaos, a refreshing of your spirit as you behold the truth and greatness of Who I Am.

While at My table, you'll also discover the truth of who you are. I only speak into your true identity.

My Beloved, shame and condemnation cannot survive at My table. They cannot linger in My Presence.

Come, Beloved, turn your focus towards Me. Pull up your chair, sit and dine with Me.

Take some time to reflect on these truths with Holy Spirit. How have you seen this in your own life and walk with God? What areas do you want to experience more of it? Ask Him to reveal more of Himself to you today.

number fifteen

1 CORINTHIANS 6:20, 1 CORINTHIANS 7:23, 2 CORINTHIANS 5:17

My Child, you are My tabernacle, bought with the steepest price. From the beginning, I desired to walk in fellowship with each and every one of My children.

Through the greatest act of love, My Son made a way for us to have this intimacy once again. You have My very DNA, Beloved. My very breath is within your lungs.

Never doubt who you are, My Child. You are a new creation. You and I are forever united together, nothing and no one can separate us.

This closeness I now have with you was worth every agonizing drop of blood poured out on Calvary—the perfect sacrifice that tore the veil separating us.

The final payment that restored you to Me. You, My Love, were worth it all.

Take some time to reflect on these truths with Holy Spirit. How have you seen this in your own life and walk with God? What areas do you want to experience more of it? Ask Him to reveal more of Himself to you today.

number sixteen

PSALM 136, PSALM 139:8, MATTHEW 6:33, NUMBERS 6:25, 1 PETER 2:24

Beloved, I need you to trust My goodness and love for you. It's unfailing and it will never waver.

So often I see My children put distance between themselves and Me when things aren't going well. This is never the answer.

I Am always the answer. If something doesn't go the way you expected, don't take the bait to turn inward and assess what you've done wrong. You will never find the truth there. I Am the Truth, seek My face.

My face shines upon you as My child. Jesus took on the shame of anything you have done or will ever do so that you would never have to bear the weight of it. Lay it down.

Don't retreat and look within, Beloved. Learn from King David's example, and instead, run to Me and seek My loving face. This is how you find your strength, by running to Me.

Take some time to reflect on these truths with Holy Spirit. How have you seen this in your own life and walk with God? What areas do you want to experience more of it? Ask Him to reveal more of Himself to you today.

number seventeen

PSALM 22:3, PSALM 100:4–5, MATTHEW 6:33

My Child, did you know that your praises become a gate I can inhabit?

It's true!

I've called you to enter My gates with praise, and to enter My courts with thankfulness. My invitation to you brings you into My Kingdom through expressions of thanksgiving and praise, and I, in turn, inhabit your praises. This exchange brings you higher above your situation, and it also brings heaven to earth.

This is why I urge you to have a thankful and hope-filled heart, your complaints are like closed doors to Me. A heart filled with hope and thankfulness cannot entertain discontentment. A mind focused on thankfulness cannot believe the lie that you lack anything. There is nothing I withhold from you, you are a co-heir with Jesus.

My Child, bring all of your cares to Me and Me alone. Let your heart lift with praise as you release your burdens into My hands. I promise I won't let you down.

Take some time to reflect on these truths with Holy Spirit. How have you seen this in your own life and walk with God? What areas do you want to experience more of it? Ask Him to reveal more of Himself to you today.

number eighteen

ROMANS 8:28, PSALM 37:5, PSALM 143:8, PROVERBS 3:5–6, LUKE 1:37, DEUTERONOMY 4:23–24

My Child, so often I've seen the fear in your heart when I ask you to give Me what you have. I want to destroy that lie right now. I cherish you and your dreams more than you do. Those dreams were bright seeds of hope I planted in your very being long before you were even a twinkle in your parents' eyes.

I thought of those dreams when I dreamed of you.

I only ask you to let Me hold your dreams so that I can protect you from creating an idol in your heart. Protecting you from the temptation to buy the lie that these dreams could fulfill what only I can do for you.

My desire for you is to magnify your ability to dream with Me and to realize that I am truly everything you will ever need. Your life unfolds with power when your heart is in proper Kingdom alignment—seeking Me first and letting everything else flow from our relationship.

I must be your first love. I am a jealous Father. I am jealous for your love.

You see now why I cannot allow these dreams to take My place in your heart, no matter how good they are?

So My Child, will you relax your grip? Will you trust Me and let go?

Take some time to reflect on these truths with Holy Spirit. How have you seen this in your own life and walk with God? What areas do you want to experience more of it? Ask Him to reveal more of Himself to you today.

number nineteen

PSALM 37:5, PSALM 143:8

My Child, trust My timing. I see the complete expanse of time, and nothing misses My gaze.

If I have you in a waiting season, it is because it is good for you to wait now. The fullness of the blessing is not ready for you just yet. To receive it too early would rob you of its fullness.

I have never and will never fail you. I will never let you down.

I'm always working My Child. Seek My face, because in My Presence you'll want for nothing.

Trust My choice to remove people and things that aren't good for you. Trust that I am working all things for your good. Cast out any fear that would attempt to tell you otherwise. My heart is, and always will be, for you.

So My Love, will you rest and trust My timing? … good, because it's always perfect.

Take some time to reflect on these truths with Holy Spirit. How have you seen this in your own life and walk with God? What areas do you want to experience more of it? Ask Him to reveal more of Himself to you today.

number twenty

JOHN 3:16–17, ROMANS 8:1 & 28

Run to Me, My Child. There is never going to be a moment in time where I would ever turn you away. No matter how difficult the situation, no matter how terrible you think something might be (behavior or otherwise), My heart towards you remains the same … deep, with all-consuming love.

I desire you to trust My heart towards you so inherently, that you never question whether or not I would receive you with arms wide open. I desire for you to know Who I Am, and Who I want to be for you.

There will never be anything you could bring Me that we cannot tackle together. There is no occurrence, no difficulty, nothing on this earth could ever be too difficult for Me to redeem. It's Who I Am. It's My heart for you.

I'm here always, My Love, with arms wide open ready to receive you in every way possible.

Take some time to reflect on these truths with Holy Spirit. How have you seen this in your own life and walk with God? What areas do you want to experience more of it? Ask Him to reveal more of Himself to you today.

number twenty one

MATTHEW 18:18, PSALM 139:14

My Child, you were never created to act as a thermometer, walking into a space and taking the temperature of the room. No, My Love, you were created for so much more than that!

As My chosen vessel, My Spirit goes with you everywhere. And with My power within you, together we can shift atmospheres. You, Beloved, were created to be a thermostat! You bring My Presence with you.

As you enter a room, you bring peace.

As you enter a room, you bring Kingdom authority.

As you enter a room, you bring the love of Christ.

My Child, when you enter a room, you bring so much more than your wonderfully made self; you bring the possibilities of Heaven invading earth. Carry it with confidence and light the world on fire.

Take some time to reflect on these truths with Holy Spirit. How have you seen this in your own life and walk with God? What areas do you want to experience more of it? Ask Him to reveal more of Himself to you today.

number twenty two

HEBREWS 6:18–20

My Child, the moment you grabbed hold of the hope I set before you, I anchored you—firm and secure. I AM your Anchor and you are My Beloved. You are blessed and highly favored.

This is your truth. Regardless of what chaos is happening out in the world, what you see with your physical eyes—those things are not the truth. They are distractions to pull you away from Kingdom-focused thinking, from keeping your mind anchored on things above.

When fear tries to distract you, set your mind on Who you are anchored to—Me, Perfect Love.

When the situation before looks like it is impossible, that there is no way through; set your mind on Who you are anchored to—Me, your God in Whom NOTHING is impossible.

When promises seem to be delayed and you are tempted to partner with doubt, set your mind on Who you are anchored to—Me, My Word NEVER returns to Me void.

You are anchored Beloved, now anchor your mind on Me.

Take some time to reflect on these truths with Holy Spirit. How have you seen this in your own life and walk with God? What areas do you want to experience more of it? Ask Him to reveal more of Himself to you today.

number twenty three

EZEKIEL 36:26, ACTS 2

The moment you responded with open arms and a hungry heart to My pursuit of you, I gave you a brand new heart and a new Spirit … MY Spirit!

My Holy Spirit came to live inside of you—to help you, guide you, comfort you, to teach you and usher you into all truth about the deep things of My heart. Oh, how I desire for you to seek out the depths of My heart!

My Spirit is your Helper, renewing your mind to think Kingdom thoughts. To see the impossible as possible because of Who I Am, and My desire to work in and through you.

Ask the Holy Spirit to fill you to overflowing so you can pour out My love on others. Ask Him to come and baptize you in power and holy refining fire, just like the day of Pentecost in the upper room.

Revival begins with just one burning heart to see heaven come to earth. Let's start it in you.

Take some time to reflect on these truths with Holy Spirit. How have you seen this in your own life and walk with God? What areas do you want to experience more of it? Ask Him to reveal more of Himself to you today.

number twenty four

JOHN 3:16–17, JOHN 19:30; ROMANS 8:1–4

My Love, the cross was— is—and always will be ENOUGH. I fulfilled every prophecy; every sin and iniquity was cast upon Me and I took it into death with Me. Its power over you died that very moment it entered into the grave with Me. Those chains are broken, let them fall.

To fear them is to partner with unbelief, saying that what I've accomplished is not enough for what you bring to the table. But Beloved, what you fail to realize in your heart is that I saw you—every single moment of your life—as I hung there on that cross and I joyfully embraced it all because I knew that it would open up the door for a relationship with you. Not even your deepest darkest sins or thoughts could turn My love away from your face.

I took it all upon Myself. I paid every single cost so that you could be free. Step out of the cage of condemnation, My Child. I destroyed the lock on that door—it no longer has the power to hold you hostage.

I see you, My Love, and I call you blessed—beautiful—and highly favored.

You are Mine and I don't regret that, not once. Not ever.

Take some time to reflect on these truths with Holy Spirit. How have you seen this in your own life and walk with God? What areas do you want to experience more of it? Ask Him to reveal more of Himself to you today.

number twenty five

JOHN 14:12, LAMENTATIONS 3:23

My Child, every new day is exactly that—brand new. Not just for you, but My mercies towards you. They are new every morning, and they never run out.

Each new day brings unlimited possibilities. My desire for you is that you wake up with great expectation of what I have planned for you!

An expectant heart is like a magnet for miracles.

An expectant heart sees the possible in the seemingly impossible.

An expectant heart is a highway for heaven to invade earth.

My Child, I am a miracle-working God and I want nothing more than to work them through you.

Take some time to reflect on these truths with Holy Spirit. How have you seen this in your own life and walk with God? What areas do you want to experience more of it? Ask Him to reveal more of Himself to you today.

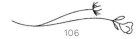

number twenty six

ROMANS 8:2 & 8:17, EPHESIANS 1:18, JOHN 8:36, 1 PETER 2:9, CORINTHIANS 5:17

My Child, you are no longer bound by the curse of sin and death. You are free!

You are a co-heir of My Kingdom, everything is yours—now. Not later down the road - not once you behave a certain way— nope, it's yours—now!

So walk tall with confidence that ALL of heaven backs you. Change your way of thinking to reflect the true citizenship to which you belong. You are made new, brand new, and you are called blessed and highly favored, redeemed and righteous. You are the head and not the tail, and it's all because you placed your faith in Me.

My victory of the cross completed the requirements for all of your sin [past/present/future]. So stop trying to earn My gifts I give freely to you out of love. All I want is to see you walk in fullness like you were always meant to.

I want to see My Children, My Royal Priesthood, bring heaven to earth.

Take some time to reflect on these truths with Holy Spirit. How have you seen this in your own life and walk with God? What areas do you want to experience more of it? Ask Him to reveal more of Himself to you today.

number twenty seven

GENESIS 2:4–3:34, JOHN 3:16, JOHN 14:6

My Child, take a walk with Me. This was My greatest joy during the cool of the day with Adam and Eve, strolling through the garden together as friends.

Our relationship, yours and Mine, is just as perfect. It has the opportunity to be just as intimate—even more so. You've been completely restored to your original intent and design. The chasm is gone. It's now you and Me, face to face.

Let this be the start of our daily strolls together. Each step a new experience. Each word a conversation between two friends, an exchange of heartbeats, as we dream together as one. There are so many amazing things I see for you!

So Beloved, here I stand with My hand outstretched. Will you take a walk with Me?

Take some time to reflect on these truths with Holy Spirit. How have you seen this in your own life and walk with God? What areas do you want to experience more of it? Ask Him to reveal more of Himself to you today.

number twenty eight

COLOSSIAN 1:9–10, JAMES 1:5, PSALM 1, PROVERBS 3:5–6, PROVERBS 4:5–9

My Child, did you know that I want you to ask Me for understanding? I don't expect you to just 'figure it out'. Relationships don't work that way.

When you seek understanding, you will gain understanding. It's the same with wisdom, if you ask for it, I will pour it out in great measure—covering you with grace. It's My promise to you!

Your life led by Me is a life filled with understanding of My will. A life that produces every good fruit. A life that takes you into greater intimacy of experiencing Me.

Seek Me first, and ask Me for understanding, Beloved. It is yours, and so am I.

Take some time to reflect on these truths with Holy Spirit. How have you seen this in your own life and walk with God? What areas do you want to experience more of it? Ask Him to reveal more of Himself to you today.

number twenty nine

ISAIAH 55:11, JOSHUA 1:9, DEUTERONOMY 31:8, PROVERBS 3:5–6, COLOSSIANS 3:2–3, JEREMIAH 29:11

My Child, My Word never returns to Me void. Once it is spoken, it is released with every ounce of power and provision to see it accomplished. So why do you hesitate?

I've called you higher, to a life victoriously lived above fear. A life filled with adventures and the miraculous, you do not need to succumb to fear.

I go before you always! My Word goes before you.

There is not one step along this path I have not accounted for. Have great faith, Beloved. Grab ahold of Me, the Way-maker, as we fulfill the words spoken over your life. I will see it through, and I've chosen to partner with you. You won't go forward alone.

My Voice will never contradict My written Word. Trust in Me with all your heart, I will make your paths straight.

Take some time to reflect on these truths with Holy Spirit. How have you seen this in your own life and walk with God? What areas do you want to experience more of it? Ask Him to reveal more of Himself to you today.

number thirty

JOHN 8:32,35–36

My Child, let go of religion's rules, the truth is not a concept. No, Beloved, the Truth is a Person calling out to be known and that Person is Me.

I Am calling you into deeper intimacy with Me. I'm calling you to experience My Presence.

Intimacy—"into Me you see".

To know Me is to know your true place in My family—firm and secure. Knowing you are My son or My daughter, bought at a great price.

To know Me is where true freedom is found. Chains of condemnation, sin, and death are broken and cast into the sea. Grace and mercy abound in the depths of My love.

To know Me is to follow My teachings with the power of My Holy Spirit. No need for striving. There's an ease in this intimacy with Me as you become familiar with your NEW self.

Come deeper into the waters of relationship, My Child. Then you will know the Truth and the Truth will set you free.

Take some time to reflect on these truths with Holy Spirit. How have you seen this in your own life and walk with God? What areas do you want to experience more of it? Ask Him to reveal more of Himself to you today.

number thirty one

MY LOVE LETTER TO THE LORD

Father, how do I even begin to explain the voyage into the depths of Your heart?

How can I, a Daughter, begin to encapsulate the majesty and wonder of Your relentless love and pursuit towards me?

The thought of attempting something so grand overwhelms my senses and abilities to string words together. And yet, I know it's a story that needs to be told … a testament to Your faithfulness, kindness, forgiveness, and goodness towards me. So I have decided to approach this in the only way I know how, by penning a love letter to You.

In my earliest memories, I remember how You introduced Yourself to me. You had given me hazel green eyes that were always wide open and full of wonder. Bright white hair and freckles that looked like You had painted them across my rosy cheeks and nose. You had placed a desire in me to be outside as often as I could, and it was there that You started to whisper my name.

Through the glistening light off of the snow-covered ground that gave the appearance of a field of diamonds waiting to be scooped up and thrown into the air. And the delicate unique details of every snowflake that would fall on my face as I stared up into the cloud-covered sky with my tongue out just trying to see what they might taste like.

You'd mesmerize me with Your brush strokes as You'd paint the evening sky with bright oranges, pinks, and yellows; every night a different design and each one a masterpiece to treasure in my heart.

The creativity of the trees that surrounded my childhood home, each one its own sense of matchless beauty. Some had grey-blue pointy leaves that never wavered regardless of the season, and every spring would produce beautiful pine cones that made the Christmas season last just a little bit longer. Then there were the ash trees that would shade me from the bright hot summer sun with its proud full canopy of dark green leaves that would soon change to fiery orange and yellow as the autumn season approached. The maples would display their royal crown of dark purple leaves all summer long and then shout to the world how beautiful they were with their big wide bright red leaves that were always my favorite to collect and sketch with my colored pencils.

You wowed my senses in my own backyard as a child, and I hadn't even seen a fraction of what You created yet. Even still, on that corner lot in a small town in Iowa, I saw You in each glorious creative detail and the wooing of my heart began.

As I began to attend Sunday School and go through all of the sacraments as a child, my awe and wonder of You only grew. I didn't have the best understanding of how to begin a relationship with Someone so magnanimous, but I approached You the best way my young, obedient heart knew how…cautiously. I didn't want to push You away (Oh how little I understood You and Your unrelenting love then haha).

I did everything that I was told to do: I read Your Word, prayed, confessed my sins, said a bunch of Hail Mary's, attended church every Sunday and tried to be nice to everyone (including my siblings). And I did, I read Your Word every night in my picture Bible that I "borrowed" from my sister since she wasn't reading it. The stories of You interacting with Your people amazed me, I couldn't get enough of it. Your dramatic rescues and awe-inspiring miracles, even the eventual disciplinary events showed me a new bit of Your nature. And it was there in those pages that a new layer of communication began between us. You lit a fire—a hunger in my heart and it continues still to this day.

This was also the time that I began to establish a prayer life with You. I still don't know how You didn't fall over laughing with the way I would hide under my bed and pray to You in King James English for the first two years of our conversations. Or when I was under that same bed and told You I would devote my entire life to serving You and I heard You say a resounding "Yes, I accept"…and I subsequently began to beg You not to make me become a Nun. A beautiful and worthy calling, but even then I knew I just wasn't designed for that life. I loved fashion (still do) and I dreamed to get married one day. You enduring my silliness just reveals to me another facet of Your Father's heart. You love to laugh with me.

You have always been as constant as a rushing river. You are the solid rock, in my life. Even in the season where I forgot my pledge to You that I made under that daybed, and instead stopped seeking You in the things that were happening in my life. The consistency of Your pursuit was never dependent on me. Rather, it has always been fully dependent on You and Your deep love for me.

For instance when the bullying began in my childhood years. While my situation didn't change until I graduated high school; You were the One strengthening my frame and shielding my thoughts from turning down a dangerous road so many of my classmates had wandered down. You were the One who (within the last three years) broke through the lie I believed from years of the verbal taunts and proclamations that I was "fat and ugly". Partnering with this lie had eventually developed into years of body shaming and seeking verbal affirmation from guys who saw me as an object and not as a woman with value or substance. This empty void eventually lead me into the three-year relationship of continuous verbal abuse and broken trust with my first boyfriend. By the time this relationship ended, I was a shell of the bright eyed girl You first met. So innocent and full of wonder was replaced with fear and shame and so much emptiness.

I only knew deep depression and self-loathing at that point in my life, and yet You never left me. Even if I didn't see you then in that season, I see You in it now. You were whispering to my heart daily to run, to get out, to stay strong and believe I was meant for more than this. You kept the small embers in my heart alive that always carried such a deep 'knowing' of a purpose greater than myself. But I didn't recognize that voice as You. I just didn't believe that You would still love me after I gave away such a precious gift You'd given me to a guy who didn't deserve it. I bought the lie of condemnation and beat myself up daily because of it. This is why I stayed because I didn't know who else would want someone that beat down and broken. Someone who, in her own eyes, was hideous to lay eyes upon. I guess when you hear the same story every day for the majority of your life, you begin to see through that lens.

Then a man (a man I knew) showed me exactly how worthless he perceived me to be by slipping something into my drink and having his way with me in the shadows of his friend's bedroom. And in the throes of the darkest day of my life, I laid shaking on my bed staring at the ceiling fan as the blades of the fan and my thoughts whirled around in circles together in unison. The clinking of the silver ball chain hitting against the frosted glass of the suspended light cover setting a rhythm for my tears as they fell down my face. And as my thoughts were threatening to take me under I reached desperately for the brown leather-bound Bible lying next to my bed. My fingers clasped the binding and pulled it in so tightly I thought it might be swallowed by my heaving chest. And it was then that I experienced Your manifest Presence for the very first time.

As I squeezed Your Word tightly to my chest, my arms pleading for the Words to wash away the fear and shame—You —the Living Word—moved into the room. You entered my room like a soft inviting blanket of comfort accompanied by cleansing showers of peace. Slowly—gently—You laid down next to me and wrapped Yourself around me and soothed my anxious thoughts and fears. The pit of loneliness that threatened to swallow me that night was defeated by my Comforter, my Rescuer, my Redeemer. And while the reality of what happened didn't disappear, You overwhelmed the heaviness of it all. For the next few months, You laid there with me every night easing my thoughts and soothing me to sleep as I clung to Your Word.

I wish this was where my heart realized that a single pursuit of You is what it was created for. I wish this was the turning point where I shouted my testimony of Your goodness from the rooftops, but it wasn't. My shame was still so deep. And yet You were faithful even then, as I continued to allow fear and shame to cloud the miraculous experience I had with You in my room for months on end.

I kept the dark secret of that violation of my body locked away inside me for years, never telling a single soul. And in that dark vault, it began to spread like a cancer, creating anxiety attacks and irrational fear to the point that I was afraid to leave my home. Still, You were there, pursuing my heart, refusing to leave me where I was—calling me higher. I see how You placed strategic people in my path that had a relationship with You that were able to infiltrate the barriers I'd placed around myself to protect me from any further trauma.

Each one would love me where I was, and gently remind me of Your true nature as a loving Father. And through each exchange, and seed of truth scattered in the garden of my heart, You slowly inched me closer and closer to the moment when You knew my heart was ready. The moment when my heart understood that all my life I had sought You out for what You could do for me and not for who You are.

It was there at the age of 27, in that sanctuary of a non-denominational church in a nearby city where I grew up, that I let go and surrendered it all. It was the very first weekend I attended there, You sat on the platform and spoke directly to my heart through the Pastor You'd appointed to be Your messenger for me that day. You overwhelmed me with Your compassion and enthusiasm to show me that You had been waiting for me to run to You all this time.

In Your Presence, there was no condemnation. None. Not even in the expressed waiting period of how long I took to turn to You. You simply ran straight at me and scooped me into Your arms as if I had never left. You held me so tightly and whispered Your adoration towards me in my ears and broke off the lies that You were ever once disappointed in me. Your unrelenting love broke through my walls and I crumbled in the best way possible.

It was then that I knew You were what my heart has longed for all my life. The last decade has taught me so much about what my life can be like every day by simply walking it out with You. Every encounter is a new layer of depth in our relationship. You're no longer an add on in my life like I treated You so long ago. You are my life, the center of it all.

The way I live each day is learning to be aware of Your Presence. Laying down my agenda so I can jump in with You and what You are doing. Do I get it right every time? Nope. But I know You delight in my trying. You keep showing me that when I fully let go and rest in You, there's no need to strive or slip back into old mindsets that died all those years ago with my old self.

You keep showing me over and over that I don't need to earn or perform for Your love; that You are absolutely smitten with everything about me because I Am Yours. You are teaching me what it means to truly receive all You have for me without the need to repay. To receive because I understand You want to shower me with Your blessing because it's a part of Your nature and You delight in me.

You've shown me that You want me to ask You questions! And I've seen You time and time again, eagerly point me towards the answers. To try and explain what I'm experiencing with You right now as You show me what it means to live fully in my NEW identity You bought for me, is difficult. I truly don't think I can put words to describe this season of acceleration in my faith until I'm looking back on it with You in a year or two. It's wild, peace-filled, and beautiful all at the same time.

One thing is certain, every time I've ever been tempted to replace You with something good, Your Shepherd heart gently convicts me and course corrects my focus. The history we've etched in my heart together reminds me You're greater. You are the true prize, and everything else doesn't require my 'hustle' or striving. It is Your great pleasure to bring it into my life as my character grows and I have the capacity to steward Your blessings well. Every trial we've faced together has shown me a new facet of Your nature and character. It's as if the trial opens up the opportunity for the child-like, wide-eyed girl inside of me to seek out what characteristic of Your nature is available to discover and experience. More of You is always the goal.

The truth is, You won't ever leave me nor forsake me. You only have good intentions towards me. So the hard stuff only shows me how unshakable one can become with You as their anchor. You are the Great I Am—You are the answer to everything I will ever face. And You are the Truth that set me free.

You make me brave when I want to retreat. You give me value/purpose and worth. You healed my heart, helped me forgive when I never thought I could, and You taught me how to love again. I know I will never feel more beautiful than the way You make me feel when I sit in Your Holy Presence and You speak Your words over me ...

The one I love calls to me:

Arise, my dearest. Hurry, my darling.
Come away with me!
I have come as you have asked
to draw you to my heart and lead you out.
For now, is the time, my beautiful one.

The season has changed,
the bondage of your barren winter has ended,
and the season of hiding is over and gone.
The rains have soaked the earth—

and left it bright with blossoming flowers.
The season for singing and pruning the vines has arrived.
I hear the cooing of doves in our land,
filling the air with songs to awaken you
and guide you forth.

Can you not discern this new day of destiny
breaking forth around you?
The early signs of my purposes and plans
are bursting forth.
The budding vines of new life
are now blooming everywhere.
The fragrance of their flowers whispers,
"There is change in the air."
Arise, my love, my beautiful companion,
and run with me to the higher place.
For now is the time to arise and come away with me.

For you are my dove, hidden in the split-open rock.
It was I who took you and hid you up high
in the secret stairway of the sky.
Let me see your radiant face and hear your sweet voice.
How beautiful your eyes of worship
and lovely your voice in prayer.

You must catch the troubling foxes,
those sly little foxes that hinder our relationship.
For they raid our budding vineyard of love
to ruin what I've planted within you.
Will you catch them and remove them for me?
We will do it together.

Song of Songs 2:10–15

(TPT–The Passion Translation)

You've completely undone me.

I am beginning to see how You have taken such awful things and are using them for good. If my story of paralyzing fear and shame to healing freedom can help just one person, then I will shout it from the mountain tops. I'm not afraid anymore.

Because the truth is, what I have—I want for everyone. I have the greatest gift I've ever known … You, my Redeemer that chased me down. My Rescuer who never once gave up on this foolish and formerly tattered heart of mine.

I have You. My Forever Friend. My Jesus, who loved me back to life.

I'm eternally Yours.

Tiffany

Made in the USA
Middletown, DE
17 November 2019